A NOTE TO PARENTS:

We hope the camping hints and safety information in this book will be helpful to parents and children alike. We have tried to show children what is appropriate to their age and abilities, but there is no substitute for the counsel of a parent in actual hiking and camping situations. We especially want to remind readers that Smokey is a special bear, and children should be cautioned to stay away from all wild animals.

Smokey Bear's Camping Book

by Irwin Shapiro
illustrated by Mel Crawford

gb GOLDEN PRESS • NEW YORK

Western Publishing Company, Inc.
Racine, Wisconsin

The Peterson family had just arrived at the
National Forest and set up their tent. Soon a Forest
Ranger brought their camping guide, Smokey Bear,
to meet them. Karen and Karl Peterson were excited,
for Smokey promised to stay and teach them how to
live in his home, the forest.

"Look, Smokey," said Karl, "our tent is just like a house. I wish we could live here all the time."

"It does look cozy," said Smokey, peeking in.

Mr. and Mrs. Peterson had brought a large tent so that the family could all fit into it. Smokey would sleep outside, warm in his fur.

Using a slide on the tent line will keep the line taut, but make it easy to adjust if necessary.

two half hitches

slide

peg

90°

"Come on!" Karen shouted. "Let's unpack our stuff so we can get started camping."

"Fine," said Smokey. "We can check it out and make sure you have everything you need." He was always happy and excited before a camping trip, too, and eager to see if everything was there.

They laid all the things they had brought out on
the ground.

"I hope we didn't forget anything," Karen said.

"I don't think so," Smokey said.

lucky stone

camp stove

matches

stove fuel

rope

pail

FIRST AID

flashlight

ice chest

thermos jug

clothing

SMOKEY

air mattress

"We did forget something!" Karl burst out.
"My trumpet!"
Karen made a face.
"That's lucky for the other campers," she said,
and Smokey laughed.

The Petersons showed Smokey their hiking clothes.

Mrs. Peterson thought her jacket might be too warm. "But if I take it off, I'm too cool. I just can't win," she told Smokey.

"Well," said Smokey, "it helps me to wear clothes in layers—like two shirts and a sweater. When I feel warm, I take off a layer or two. When I feel cool, I put on a layer or two."

"Oh, neat!" said Karl.

"And, by the way," Smokey said. "Never go on a hike with shoes that aren't broken in—I've seen lots of people make that mistake, and were they sorry!"

YOU'LL PROBABLY NEED MOST OF THESE ...

Cotton Shirts

Jeans

Sturdy Shoes for Hiking

Sneakers

Wool Socks

Cotton Socks

Wool Sweaters

Underwear

Handkerchiefs

Swim Trunks

Swim Suit

Poncho for Rainy Weather

They started to stow the equipment away.
Smokey told Karen and Karl to put the bread, flour,
sugar, cereal, and fruit in a large sack. Then he tied
a long rope to the sack, and hung it over the high
limb of a tree.

"There," he said. "Now your food is safe from
ground animals, and the tin can will even keep the
squirrels out of it."

The Petersons were hot from their long drive and their work setting up camp. So everyone went for a dip in the lake near the campsite.

Smokey wondered if the children could swim.

"Sure we can. We took a class last winter," said Karl. "They taught us the crawl and the breaststroke."

"That's great," said Smokey. "Hey, look at that family in the boat! They look like they're having a good time."

"So are we!" said Karen, cannonballing into the water.

HERE ARE SMOKEY'S WATER TIPS!

Always swim with a buddy. Dive in deep water only.

Don't stand up in a boat.

If boat tips over, hang on and wait.

Wait an hour after eating before you swim.

Use suntan lotion to avoid sunburn.

If you can't swim, always wear a life jacket when playing in or near the water.

Even if you can swim, always wear a life jacket in a boat.

After getting dressed, Smokey, Karen and Karl took a walk. They saw three hikers.

"They don't have a car, or anything," Karen said.

"That's right," Smokey said, nodding. "They're backpacking—carrying everything on their own backs. Let's go talk to them."

The hikers showed Karen and Karl the things they carried in their packs.

"Is that all you need?" asked Karl.

"Sure," said one of the backpackers, "you'd be surprised how little you really need if you know how to get along in the woods. This is all the three of us are taking for a whole week."

explorer tent

backpack

camp stove

flashlight

waterproof match
container

whetstone

knife

cooking & eating kit

sleeping bag

compass

hatchet

canteen

first aid kit

dried food

contour map

change of clothing

USE
FIRE WITH
CAUTION

On their way back to their own campsite, Karl
and Karen and Smokey saw many different kinds
and sizes of tents.

19

They also saw people driving in with different
kinds of camping trailers. They looked into one
of them.

"Wow!" said Karl. "This is really like a house!"

Karen said, "It doesn't seem much like
camping to me."

"Well, some people don't like the bother of
putting up a tent and cooking over a fire," said
Smokey. "Live and let live, I always say," he added
with a smile.

That evening Smokey invited the children to go
on an overnight backpacking trip with him the next
day. "All you will need to pack will be your canteens,
a change of clothes, and a blanket each," said
Smokey. "I'll take care of the food and anything else."

So Karen and Karl excitedly packed their
knapsacks. It was dark when they finally crawled
into their sleeping bags, and they could hear the
sound of their parents and Smokey softly talking
around the campfire.

Early the next morning, Smokey came to the Peterson's campsite.

"Good morning, Smokey," Mr. Peterson said. "What a fine day for a hike—not too warm, not too cool!"

"I don't care if it's warm or cool," Karl said. "I've got my clothes on in layers, the way you told Mommy."

"So have I," said Karen.

"Good. Are your canteens filled with water?" asked Smokey.

"Right up to the top," Karen answered.

"Then we're all set. Let's go!" said Smokey.

And, waving to Mr. and Mrs. Peterson, he and Karen and Karl set off along the trail.

They went deeper and deeper into the woods.
Karl looked around, puzzled.

"It's kind of hard to see the trail," he said.
"How do we know we're not lost?"

"Haven't you noticed that some of the trees
have a white spot on the trunk?" said Smokey.
"The Forest Rangers painted those to mark the trail."

"Oh, so we just follow the marks, and we can't
get lost," said Karen.

"Oops! I almost forgot something," Smokey said.

He gave Karen and Karl each a little whistle on a string. "If you should lose the trail," he said, "don't keep on walking. Stay in the same place and blow your whistle. Someone will find you."

Karen and Karl did a little practice whistling.

THINGS TO REMEMBER SO YOU DON'T GET LOST!

Always take an adult when you go into the woods.

Stay together and stay on the trail.

24

"I hope it doesn't rain," Karl said.

"Well, rain or shine," said Smokey, "it's all part of camping. But I'm pretty sure it won't rain today."

"How can you tell?" asked Karen.

"There are several ways to guess the weather," said Smokey, and he told them of some weather signs to look for. He loved showing Karen and Karl the woods.

Dew on grass in the morning usually means fair weather.

HERE ARE MORE OF SMOKEY'S WEATHER SIGNS.

Smoke rising straight up usually means fair weather.

Red sky in the morning usually means rainy weather.

Smoke turning downward usually means stormy weather.

Red sky in the evening usually means fair weather.

LOOK! SOME IMPORTANT TIPS ON FIRST AID!

1. For blisters—to keep a blister from breaking, cover it with an adhesive bandage.

2. For insect stings—apply baking soda mixed with water. (Mud also cools painful stings.)

3. For a sprained ankle—put bandage over shoe to keep swelling down.

Suddenly Karen let out a yell. She hopped up and down and waved her arms.

"What's eating you?" Karl asked.

"Mosquitoes, that's what!" she said, and began to dance around again.

"Let's put on the insect repellant," said Smokey. "That should keep those bugs away."

As they walked through a clearing, Karl reached out his hand to pick some leaves off a plant. Quickly, Smokey grabbed his arm and pulled him back.

It was poison ivy. Smokey showed the children the clusters of three shiny leaves and the white berries. He told them that poison ivy, poison oak, and poison sumach could give them terrible itching and blisters. "If you do happen to touch them, wash well with soap and water, and put on calamine lotion," he cautioned them. He also told them never to eat anything they found growing in the woods.

poison ivy

poison oak

poison sumach

At lunchtime they stopped to rest. They had a sandwich lunch. They drank water from their canteens. Then they went on again.

Later in the afternoon, Smokey stopped.

"This looks like a good place to camp," he said. "It's nice and level. It's not too near a swamp or tall grass, so we won't get too many insects. And we can get water from the stream."

They made two A-tents out of tarpaulins and strong sticks—
one tent for Smokey, one for Karen and Karl.

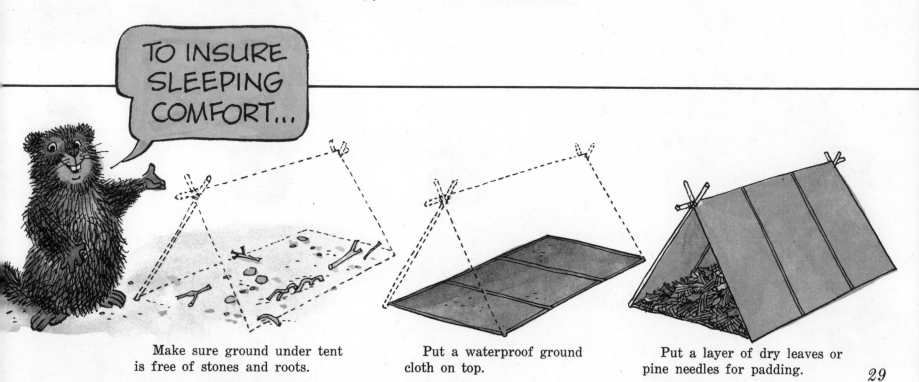

TO INSURE SLEEPING COMFORT...

Make sure ground under tent is free of stones and roots.

Put a waterproof ground cloth on top.

Put a layer of dry leaves or pine needles for padding.

Instead of using sleeping bags, they made beds out of blankets.

"I think it's good to know how to make a blanket bed," said Smokey. "On an overnight trip, when the weather is warm, you might not want to carry a big sleeping bag."

HERE'S A WAY TO MAKE A COMFORTABLE BED!

ZZZZZZ

"You know something?" Karl said. "My stomach
is growling for food."

"I'm hungry, too," Karen said.

"So am I," said Smokey. "I'm as hungry as a—
well, as a bear."

They all laughed together.

"Let's get supper started," said Smokey. "First
we need wood for a fire. The best kind is the dry
dead branches you find on the ground. They burn
really well."

Smokey showed them a good way to make a campfire for cooking.

HERE ARE THREE MORE WAYS TO MAKE A FIREPLACE.

Rock Fireplace

Make two rows, close enough together to hold pots and pans.

Keyhole Fireplace

Lay fire in rock-lined hole. Good for cooking and storytelling.

Hunter's Fireplace

Forked sticks for pot hangers.

Lay fire between two logs. Build frame for hanging pots.

"I'm going to get some water from the stream," Karen said. "I'm thirsty."

"Yes, so am I," Smokey said, "but we can't be sure the water in the stream is drinkable, even though it looks clean. We'll have to boil it first, then let it cool. It takes a long time, but we won't get sick if we do it."

ANOTHER WAY TO PURIFY WATER IS TO GET *HALAZONE* TABLETS FROM A DRUG STORE, PUT 2 TABLETS IN A QUART OF WATER, LET IT STAND FOR HALF AN HOUR.

By this time, they were all VERY hungry.
They cooked dinner over the fire—camper's stew and
twist bread. Everybody ate a lot. They decided to
save their dried fruit and chocolate bars for a
bedtime snack.

Twist Bread Recipe

Take two fistfuls of flour,
two 2-finger pinches of salt,
two 2-finger pinches of baking soda,
two 1-finger gobs of fat, and
enough water to make dough stiff.
Form into long sausage and
twist around stick. Bake
over glowing coals.

After eating, they cleaned up. Smokey poured
water on the fire to put it out. Karen poked the ashes
with a stick to make sure not one spark was left.

Sitting quietly a little way from camp, they watched for animals. As twilight fell, they saw a rabbit nibbling the grass on the other side of the stream. A raccoon began to come down from a tree. A deer walked cautiously out of the woods, carefully approached the water, and began to drink. Then Karen scratched her mosquito bite, and the animals ran away into the forest.

When night came, they made a small fire.

"A campfire doesn't have to be big," Smokey told the children. "You can keep just as warm if you sit near a little one."

The three friends sat close around the campfire, singing songs and telling stories.

Soon, Karen began to yawn. So did Smokey.
So did Karl.

"I don't know about you, but I'm getting sleepy,"
yawned Smokey.

They made sure the fire was out, then crawled
into their tents. Soon they were fast asleep.

In the morning, after breakfast, they cleaned up the campsite. They burned whatever trash they could, and put the rest in a plastic bag.

"We'll dump it in a trash can when we get back to the campground," Smokey said.

They packed their things and started back along the trail. It was getting windy.

Soon they heard thunder. The wind blew, and
dark clouds filled the sky. It started to sprinkle.

"Hey, I'm getting wet," shouted Karl.

"No! Come back!" Smokey called. "Under a tree
is the worst place in a thunderstorm!"

Smokey led them to shelter under an overhanging
rock. They were just in time. The rain poured down.
Lightning flashed in the sky.

"Look!" gasped Karen.

"Wow! I see what you mean about trees being dangerous!" Karl said.

Smokey nodded. He told them that if they were ever caught out in the open in a thunderstorm, they should lie down flat on the ground. They would feel exposed, but they would be safer than under a tree.

THESE ARE SAFE PLACES IN A THUNDER-STORM!

in a cave

in a ditch or hollow

lying flat in an open field

Soon the storm was over.

"The sky is clearing," said Karl, looking up.

"Look out!" shouted Smokey, trying to catch
him as he stumbled over a rock.

"Clumsy!" Karen said. The next minute she
slipped on some wet leaves and fell to the ground.

"Ha!" said Karl. "Who's clumsy now?"

Smokey smiled and said, "You're not clumsy—
just a little careless. It's always a good rule to watch
where you're going in the woods. It's even more
important after a rain. You can easily slip on a wet
rock or wet leaves."

In the afternoon, Smokey, Karen, and Karl
reached the Peterson's campsite.

"Mommy! Daddy!" Karl yelled. "We're back!
We learned a lot about camping!"

"We had a super time," said Karen.

"So did I!" said Smokey.

44

After supper, all the Petersons said goodbye to Smokey and promised they would be back to visit him. Smokey waved to them as he disappeared into the forest.

"See you next summer," he called.